ONE-ON-ONE
WITH A MOM OF A SPECIAL-NEEDS CHILD

Six Key Strategies for
Victorious Caregiving

Bobbie Lynn Rider

Copyright © 2018 Bobbie Lynn Rider. All rights reserved.

No part of this publication may be reproduced, distributed, or transmitted in any form or by any means, including photocopying, recording, or other electronic or mechanical methods, without the prior written permission of the publisher, except in the case of brief quotations, embodied in reviews and certain other non-commercial uses permitted by copyright law.

Praise for *One on One with a Mom of a Special-Needs Child*

Bobbie Lynn Rider writes with a passion for serving and leading her special needs child and each member of her family. She authentically describes the joys and challenges of victorious care giving. Her experiences, insights and dependence on the Lord provide wisdom to all who are managing the diverse needs of these special households.

Susan Kehl, PhD, RN, CNE
Dean of Carr College of Nursing
Dean and Associate Professor
Harding University

Bobbie Lynn Rider has given us a very practical and spiritual guide to parenting special-needs children. Bobbie Lynn draws from her experience as the primary care-giver for her daughter with Down Syndrome. She includes some commonly asked questions parents have when given the news their child has one of the special-needs diagnoses. She then moves onto six key strategies needed for *victorious caregiving* which I found very helpful and absolutely the healthy perspective a parent must have to do this important work. Bobbie Lynn's principles are firmly built on the foundation of Scripture and spiritual principles. I especially liked her concept of whispering Jesus' name when a parent is in a challenging situation. I look forward to being able to recommend Bobbie Lynn's book to my clients and other parents with which I work.

Keith Fussell, M.A.
Licensed Professional Counselor—
Mental Health Service Provider
Licensed Marriage and Family Therapist
Christian Counseling Center of Bartlett, LLC—
Bartlett Tennessee
www.BartlettChristianCounseling.com

Dedication

To Camille, without whom I would never have lived life to the fullest.

To Danny, my best friend, my husband, my encourager, my love.

To Ellen and Davis, this is for you, so that you know, with God's help, you can dream and accomplish great things throughout your life.

To my "accountabilibuddy" and new friend Kathy Anderson, thanks for all your encouragement and accountability throughout this whole process of writing and publishing our first books.

To my church family and friends, thank you for loving me through the good, the bad, and the ugly.

To God, thank you for the blessings You continually bestow.

Words cannot express my love for You.

I am eternally grateful to know You.

Table of Contents

Preface	1
Acknowledgements	3
Introduction	7
Questions and Answers	11
Six Key Strategies for Victorious Caregiving	69
Summary	109
About the Author	115

Preface

The book you have in your hands was born out of the need to obtain much-needed answers to a myriad of questions stirring in my head when my own daughter was born with Down syndrome.

I would like to acknowledge the couple who inspired me to write down my questions and insights and share them with the world. My friends Matt and Allison have a son whom they never thought they would get to know. The doctors prepared them for the worst-case scenario. Now, however, their son is defying all odds and growing and learning and doing things they never even dreamed he would accomplish.

I remember in fall 2016, when they learned of a new diagnosis for their little boy. It was autism. Although they had their suspicions, the label and the blow hit hard. What would it mean for their family, for them

One-on-One with a Mom of a Special-Needs Child

personally? Was help available? How would they proceed?

One of my first thoughts after reading Allison's sweet and open post on social media was how I wished I could just sit down with them and answer some of their questions. I wanted to reassure them that this diagnosis was not the end at all, but rather the beginning of a new chapter in the story of their lives.

I began to write down general questions that stumped my own family when we first had our daughter. I spent the next few months pouring out my heart with what I might tell them as if we were face-to-face.

I pray this book might be a Godsend to anyone facing a difficult diagnosis. Finding out that your child, parent, sibling, or friend has a disability can be heartwrenching, but it can also lead to joy unending and love you never dreamed possible.

I want to personally thank you, Matt and Allison, for your honest and open hearts in sharing your story and your lives with all of us. This transparency is much needed in a day and time when people need hope. Your story is an inspiration to many.

Acknowledgements

I would like to acknowledge my editor, Susan Thurman Houchin. I met Susan our first week at the University of Tennessee as freshmen. She has been a dear friend and sister in Christ since that time.

Susan, you have a gift with the English language that few possess. Your passion to help others with the written word is awesome. I could never have finished my book and the process of writing and editing without your assistance. I am thankful for your insight and knowledge and your honesty.

I would like to sincerely thank my new friend Grace Ostdiek for her work on my book cover. She was able to take what was in my head and make it appear on paper. It turned out amazingly beautiful. You are the best!

One-on-One with a Mom of a Special-Needs Child

I want to thank some of my friends. Angie Langley and Sherri Guyette, I have always said that if I ever get to speak on my life as a mom with a special-needs child that you guys would never be allowed to attend. Why? Because you might just heckle me during the inspirational talk since you lived through the good, the bad, and the ugly! You both have seen me through thick and thin, listened to me complain and whine, and encouraged me when I was down.

Sue Mink, my friend and mentor, you have been there, done that, and have the t-shirt. You have always championed my daughter and helped me out more than I deserve. God has blessed me with the "sister" I never had growing up. Thank you!

To my family, Danny, Ellen (and Eli), and Davis—you lived it all with me. From the first moment we each laid eyes on Camille, we fell madly in love with her. Yes, she has been a sassy, annoying, limelight-stealing, mess of a sister and daughter. We have watched her do things we never imagined. We have watched her love people, and in the process, she taught us how to love more fully and unconditionally.

It has been a wild ride, but I know for certain, we would never have wished for anything less.

Bobbie Lynn Rider

To my family, thank you for always loving Camille and loving us and helping us. You are simply the best.

Finally, I want to recognize some special people who passed on a legacy of love:

Margo Smith (1936 – 2014), my Mom

Robert Lee (Bobby) Brown (1935 – 2016), my Dad

Betty Sue Rider (1932 – 2014), my Mother-in-law

Thorwald Augustine (Punk) Rider (1930 – 2009), my Father-in-law

Lauraette Cheatham Morrow (1940 – 2017), my Aunt

The dash between their birth and death represents a lifetime—a lifetime of love, legacy, and hope. Each of these special people contributed to our lives in ways that taught us to persist and thrive in the face of adversity.

May we care for all those around us who need a little help, and in doing so, continue this legacy of love.

Introduction

What do you do when the doctor looks you in the eyes and tells you that your child or loved one has a disability? After the initial shock wears off and you have kicked, screamed, and cried—whether on the inside or the outside—how do you proceed? The typical, initial reaction is either information overload or a barren desert of nothingness before you. How do you tell your family and friends? Will people treat you and/or your child differently? Does anyone understand what I am going through, how I feel, and my fears for my child, my family, and myself?

I am here to reassure you that you are definitely not alone. I will come along beside you.

This book contains two distinct parts: The first part includes the most commonly asked questions for new caregivers, along with realistic and often-times

One-on-One with a Mom of a Special-Needs Child

humorous, common-sense answers. I will speak directly to your heart, and I will help you sift through the chaos to hone in on the information for your specific situation. The second part contains my six key strategies to help you build victorious caregiving skills.

These questions, answers, and strategies will help you begin to move forward. I will be a trusted friend and comrade on your special-needs journey.

As a mom to a 17-year-old daughter with Down syndrome, I offer practical advice for your everyday concerns. I have also worked with special-needs children in a school-to-work transition program. Additionally, I have a Bachelor's degree in Child and Family Studies and a Master's degree in Education, and I have successfully homeschooled my three children, the two oldest who are now in college. Besides working with my children, I helped with the care of my mom when she dealt with dementia for a period of seven years until she passed away, and I helped care for my mother-in-law when she needed extra assistance in her final years.

At the beginning of my journey as the parent of a special-needs child, I specifically recall wanting desperately to just sit down and talk with someone who had had a similar experience and who might have answers to my burning questions. I wished for a manual or guide that I could easily pick up and put down again and again for reassurance and answers to my many questions. Every one of our situations is different, but you are not alone. In the following chapters, I offer simple, humorous, proven solutions to help you on your own journey on this unique road as a caregiver of a special-needs child or individual.

I have been there, done that, and bought the t-shirt, so to speak! The answers I offer are ones that I have wrestled with on more than one occasion. I suggest strategies that have worked for my family and me; I also share ideas that did not work for us, but which may work for you in your specific special-needs situation. The confirmation will be in the smile on your face and the sense of encouragement you will feel when you explore these strategies in your own life and situation.

I promise to equip you with hope and spark joy for your special journey. You will gain a sense of resolve to meet your mountains head on and to conquer your fears. You will feel empowered to carry on by utilizing my six strategies for victorious caregiving.

One-on-One with a Mom of a Special-Needs Child

I am excited to share with you what I have learned on my over 17-year journey caring for my daughter. My wish is that by reading about my experience and strategies as a special-needs parent, your journey will be more joyous, and perhaps, a little easier.

Questions and Answers

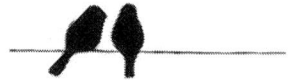

QUESTIONS

1. What do I do first?

2. What do I do next?

3. How do I find help for my caregiving situation?

4. Will my child die prematurely?

5. How do I let friends and family know about my child, and how do I educate them regarding a diagnosis? (This would apply when referring to a newborn or other-aged individual.)

6. How do I explain to my other children about my special-needs child's differences?

One-on-One with a Mom of a Special-Needs Child

7. Does this mean I will never leave the house again or have a life of my own?

8. How do I deal with social media and everyone who posts about their "perfect children and families"?

9. Can I homeschool my special-needs child?

10. Will my child learn best in a typical classroom environment or a in a self-contained learning environment in their school? How do I handle potential bullying situations?

11. Will my child have "regular" friends?

12. Will my child live a "normal" childhood?

13. As a two-parent family, how do we grow in our marriage and not allow the challenges of raising a special-needs child (or caring for special-needs loved one) strain our relationship?

14. I feel overwhelmed. What can I do to help myself?

15. Will I ever have "me" time" when I have a special-needs child?

16. Are there groups and/or support groups available for individuals who have situations like mine?

17. I have a special-needs daughter. How do I teach her about her periods?

18. How do I teach my special-needs child about sexuality?

19. I am a caregiver to an aging, special-needs individual. How do I help this person maintain his or her dignity?

20. How do I adequately care for and assist an aging parent or an elderly loved one?

ANSWERS

Question 1
What do I do first?

Now that you have a diagnosis, you need practical advice on how to proceed. These are difficult questions to consider as you help your loved one to the best of your ability.

You are not alone. All of us "special-needs parents" have been there. Please feel free to get a cup of coffee (or tea, if you prefer), and we will answer some of these challenging questions together.

As we begin, I offer you an anecdote. Our family visited the Grand Canyon several years ago. We enjoyed the park for a few days and experienced the majesty and beauty of the canyon. Having young children at the time, we knew that hiking in the canyon was not really a wise option. I remember reading all the signs posted for those interested in hiking. They were serious, and even grave, about what to expect. Hiking successfully in the canyon required certain essentials. I heard stories of people who ventured off unprepared, and because of the extreme conditions in this particular park, the details regarding their consequences were often tragic, usually resulting in their demise.

I distinctly remember going to a trailhead and seeing all the preparations being made for a hiking group ready to head out. There were guides checking their gear, mules loaded and stocked with essential equipment, and hikers dressed and prepping for their adventure.

Standing at the trailhead and looking down at the path below, I could see the first 50 yards of the path, and it looked safe enough. By peering further down, I could see bits and pieces of the trail. Off in the distance, I saw a group of hikers who looked like ants way down on the trail. With binoculars, one might possibly have been able to see a campsite near the river at the very bottom. I remember standing there and fully knowing that I was not going to hike, but just looking at the trail and knowing what comprised a safe hiking experience was truly overwhelming.

When I received the diagnosis that my mom had dementia, and when I learned that my daughter had Down syndrome, I had nearly the same experience. In my mind, I was looking down the trail, and I was frozen with terror. I was not at all prepared, nor was I willing to begin either unique journey.

Question 2
What do I do next?

Well, after crying, and possibly kicking and screaming (all this went on inside my head—probably inside yours, as well), sit down and pray. Ask God what He wants you to do with and for this unique and special child He has given you. By the way, it is okay to question and even yell at Him as needed. I promise that God can take it, I promise that He will not judge you, and I promise that He will make His will known for your child or loved one.

We found out that our daughter Camille had Down syndrome at birth. After the initial shock wore off, and she was thoroughly checked out and received a good bill of health, we proceeded to cry and talk for hours about how this was going to affect our lives. My husband and I decided right then and there that she was a blessing and that we would do everything in our power to tell others our story of hope and love for her.

We connected with a new friend who also had a young son with Down syndrome. This mom said that she and her husband sent out birth announcements with a picture of their son explaining his diagnosis and just simply welcoming him to the world and to their family and friends.

We liked this couple's idea of sending out an announcement, so that is what we did! This one, simple birth announcement changed our lives tremendously. We briefly explained our situation on our terms and let our loved ones know about Camille's special needs. We were thrilled to introduce our beautiful baby girl to everyone and let them know how much we were in love with her and looked forward to their meeting her.

The birth announcement took away an awkwardness. It immediately let everyone know about Camille and her disability, how we felt about her, and how much we wanted them to love her and get to know her, as well.

Even if your child is older when you get a diagnosis, I suggest a printed card as a helpful way to let others know. Many stores and online companies make and sell all kinds of personalized printed cards and ways to communicate that include sentiments and pictures. Sharing news in printed form with friends and loved ones acts as an icebreaker if you are not sure how to communicate your child's diagnosis. Letting people know how much you love and want to help your child

One-on-One with a Mom of a Special-Needs Child

enables others to let down their guard and be more understanding toward you and your child.

Question 3
How do I find help in my caregiving situation?

Finding assistance with caregiving for a special-needs child or adult presents challenges. In our particular situation, one of the first things my husband and I did was to find a support group. Depending on where you live and the type of diagnosis your special-needs loved one receives, finding a support group can either be simple or difficult. But, once you find and connect with a common group, it eases your mind and your anxiety. Seeing with your own eyes that others are along the path with you is extremely comforting.

While the internet is a great resource for information, actually talking in person with other parents and caregivers is often more assuring and helpful. People will tell you about other parents they know in the same or in a similar situation. Start there first. Perhaps there is a yearly convention where you can go for more help. Just jump in with both feet and keep searching until you find what works best for you and your situation.

A word of friendly advice: sometimes one or the other spouse will not be on the same page. That is okay, understandable, and quite normal. It takes time to live with and accept changes you were not expecting. Discovering what works best for each individual family member also requires reflection, patience, and understanding. If you are the parent who is either alone physically or alone emotionally dealing with your child, please find help for yourself. Pray that the other spouse will come around and get on board. God has a way of touching hearts that we just cannot reach.

Question 4
Will my child die prematurely?

Wondering whether your precious special-needs child will die prematurely is natural. I know this is kind of morbid, but it went through my mind when my daughter was first born. She was in the NICU for several days, and the medical staff was concerned that she might have heart and respiratory issues. The doctor also mentioned that children with Down syndrome have a higher rate for leukemia. "Great," I thought.

I remember feeling that my daughter was somehow more fragile in all areas, besides just her health, and I was scared about most everything at first.

Again, every diagnosis is different. According to the National Down Syndrome Society website, (ndss.org), "Life expectancy for people with Down Syndrome has increased dramatically in recent decades—from 25 in 1983 to 60 today." Most individuals simply learn to live with their own normal with no more risks than typically developing children. I actually know a man with Down syndrome who is in his 60s and who now has Alzheimer's.

One-on-One with a Mom of a Special-Needs Child

God has a plan for each life, no matter how short or how long that life may be.

Prayer is always the place to take your concerns and your petitions. God already knows our hearts and the fear and pain we sometimes carry with us. Allow Him to comfort you and give you peace concerning your loved one and your responsibilities in caring for them.

Perhaps you are the caregiver for an elderly person, a parent, a sibling, child, or a friend. This question of "Will my child or loved one die prematurely?" hits a little closer to home for you.

The most important things I learned from helping my mom was to allow her dignity and always to assume the best. A time for difficult decisions is often unavoidable, but until that day comes, help them live as productive of a life as possible. Various kinds of therapies, devices, and equipment are available, but you are their best resource and advocate.

Death is inevitable for all of us. There are no guarantees from day to day. Simply live life to the best of your ability while you have it and while your loved ones are here.

Question 5 & Question 6 Combined
How do I let friends and family know about my child, and how do I educate them regarding a diagnosis? (This would apply when referring to a newborn or other-aged individual.)

How do I explain to my other children about my special-needs child's differences?

If you start to notice a pattern here, then you are catching on quickly as to how I view and "do life". Yes, pray about this. God and His wisdom are always the first place to begin. Talk to your spouse, family members, and/or friends, and decide how to proceed. Some of you have young children who would not really understand. For some of you, your special-needs child is your firstborn, but when you do have other children, it will be necessary at some point to have a conversation.

Talk about your child's diagnosis and challenges, but mostly, talk as if it is a natural part of life and a natural part of your family. Some things will need to be explained, especially to savvy little kids. I had two older, typically developing children, and then my daughter with Down syndrome was born. As she began to grow up and needed disciplining, my others would complain, "Mom, if I had done that, you would have had a cow!", to which I would respond, "When you are older and have a child with a disability, you may discipline them as you please, but for now, this is how it is going to be."

When a child with a disability has a visual cue (such as being in a wheelchair or possessing physical attributes like those associated with having Down syndrome), then it becomes obvious to others that there are issues of some kind. However, there are disabilities where it is not quite so apparent. This can be difficult when someone outside the family reacts negatively or in an unkind way (even unintentionally) toward your special-needs child or adult. Discussing others' reactions toward or regarding your child and talking about how to respond/act appropriately to those reactions with your children and family will help. It will prepare your family and others working with your special-needs child to know what to expect, to better understand others' reactions, and to help them process their own feelings, which may include anger, resentment, and/or embarrassment. You may also instruct your children and others how best to react appropriately when someone behaves less-than hospitably toward their special-needs sibling. Everyone involved should be on board and as prepared as possible for the unexpected.

Children, even young children, are not misinformed. They are smarter than you think. It helps everyone involved when you can freely share your thoughts and feelings. Harsh things will be said out loud by others. Teaching your children about love, mercy and compassion are great ways to help everyone deal with difficult and awkward issues.

The more everyone in your family learns to deal with disability in general, the better your family will become. Your family life will be blessed by learning how to give and take, by understanding that life does not revolve only around you and your wants and desires. You should begin to see a natural inclination in your typically developing children to be attentive and caring toward others who are different. It is rather breathtaking to watch and to see this in action. It is one of God's blessings in having us deal with life's challenges.

A word of advice: The more open and honest you are with yourself and with your family, including your other children, the better you all will be able to deal with most any situation. If your loved one is terminal, talk about it. Encourage family members to discuss their thoughts and feelings. Allow emotions to flow freely. If for any reason, you just do not know what to do or say, seek help. Doctors, nurses, counselors, and

One-on-One with a Mom of a Special-Needs Child

clergy can help you or direct you to someone who can.

Question 7
Does this mean I will never leave the house again or have a life of my own?

No, you will leave your house and have a life of your own. Your life may, at times, look a little (or a lot) different from what you envisioned, and on occasion, your time out might be limited. However, your new normal will soon be more balanced and settled.

I know people who have successful careers and have a child with a disability, and I know people who give their lives wholly to serving their child. It will depend on your child's or loved one's type of disability and how much assistance they may need. At times, you may step back from your activities for a bit or leave your vocation altogether.

Caregiving has more to do with learning about yourself, and oftentimes, self-sacrifice, than just having to stay in or give up things in your life. It has more to do with serving and learning about love, mercy and compassion. That is not to say that caregivers who continue to work outside the home are not doing what they should. Instead, it is simply learning a new way of life that works for you and your loved one.

One-on-One with a Mom of a Special-Needs Child

Will your life be different? Yes. Will you at times need to give up some things to help someone you love? Yes. This is what parenting, in general, is all about anyway. Will we do everything perfectly along the way? No. Accept disability as a learning curve. Parenting children with disabilities just may be more curved than parenting typically developing children.

Question 8
How do I deal with social media and everyone else who posts about their "perfect children and families"?

Viewing social media can wreak havoc on one's self-esteem. No one has a perfect family. No one. I could show you some of my picture albums and tell you stories of what was happening right before and right after most of these pictures were taken.

For some of you, this will be a nonissue. For others, it will be difficult. For those of you who struggle, consider some lessons that I have learned.

LIFE LESSONS:

- Focus on the important and what is best for you and your family. At times, you need to wear blinders—the kind horses wear in a race. The purpose of blinders is to keep the horse focused on the goal ahead and not be distracted by what is going on around him. It is the same for people. At times, I must just focus on what I need to do and what is best for my family and not get distracted with what everyone else is doing around me.

- Learn to be thankful and grateful for where you are, what you have, and how you are doing right now. You will learn to appreciate life's sweetest and smallest accomplishments. Some of these will only be known by you and your immediate loved ones. Be like Mary, Jesus' mother. She treasured all these things in her heart. (I will discuss this more later.)

- Life is life. There is good, bad, and ugly. But, there is joy in living through difficulties and coming through them. The lessons you will learn and the things you will accomplish may appear to others as nothing special, but you will know what you have lived through.

- Be aware that social media does not always reflect reality. Social media is what it is: Media (pictures, videos, and words) shared socially. It is nothing more, nothing less. They are merely snapshots in time. You have no idea what happened just before or just after each picture. We truly do not know what someone else is living through. Just because someone is smiling on the outside, does not mean they are smiling on the inside.

- Take a break from social media. It is okay to do this from time to time—or forever.

- "Like what you got, and want what you have." This is a lesson I have tried to teach my children, and most days, I should remind myself of this. It is not the easiest lesson, but a necessary one.

- Cherish the sweet, special, and spiritual moments. The land of special needs is not all pestilence and disease. There are some difficult things, tough things, and horrible things on some days, but there are also sweet things, special things, and spiritual things on other days. Remember, someone out there always has it way worse, while someone else has it better.

- Whisper Jesus' name when you get discouraged. When I feel down, get my feelings hurt, or begin to feel sorry for myself, I just whisper His name over and over until the feelings pass. It is basically a one-word prayer to get my immediate focus back on track and not on what is going on around me.

One-on-One with a Mom of a Special-Needs Child

> Keeping my heart and mind centered on Jesus all the time is important. (I will discuss this more later.)

The point of all this is to encourage you. Your normal may not look like everyone else's normal. But, you know what? That is okay. You will figure out your new normal. One day, you will find yourself doing something you used to hate doing. You will all-of-a-sudden realize that you do not hate it anymore. You may still not like it, but you won't hate it. You will smile and realize just how far you have come, and you will be grateful for your blessings and your accomplishments.

When social media gets you down, take a break, put your blinders on, and go do something with your family that you enjoy. Take your own pictures, and choose not to share them with anyone else but your loved ones—or save them for yourself. When you look at those pictures in the future, be thankful for your loved ones and for your blessings.

Question 9
Can I homeschool my special-needs child?

You can absolutely homeschool your child with special needs! Will you always want to homeschool? Of course not! I will be the first person to tell you "If momma ain't happy, ain't nobody happy!" The decision of whether you will homeschool your child with special needs must come solely from the parent attempting homeschooling in the first place. If your heart is not in it, do not do it.

I chose to homeschool all my children. My two typically developing older children continued successfully to college. My youngest with Down syndrome is a "rising special-needs senior" this year. Our homeschool has looked different for each child. But, in the end it has always been doable for us as a family.

Many different types of curriculum exist, and I have bought several over the years. In the end, I finally realized that if I didn't like it in the first place, it did me absolutely no good to purchase it no matter how good others claimed it to be.

Many resources are available to help your child succeed. Sometimes it can be overwhelming, but you

One-on-One with a Mom of a Special-Needs Child

can also learn a lot from parents of children with special needs and from their experiences. Connecting with others is a great way to find out what works in different situations.

The bottom line is that, if you really want to homeschool, it is possible, and I have found that it is always worth the effort. However, there is nothing wrong with whichever you choose for yourself, your special-needs child, and your family. School works great for some; homeschool works great for others.

If you decide to homeschool, I highly recommend joining the Home School Legal Defense Association (HSLDA). This organization has proven to be a Godsend to many people, whether it involved special needs or not. They have attorneys and trained professionals to assist with educational questions and concerns. They even have a department solely to assist people who need advice about homeschooling children with special needs.

Question 10
Will my child learn best in a typical classroom environment or a in a self-contained learning environment in his or her school? How do I handle potential bullying situations?

The answer to this depends on where you live and how well you know your school and the staff and administration. Another factor is how well your child knows other kids in the school system. If your child is well liked and has a good relationship with most kids, then the other students may stick up for yours when needed.

The answer may also depend on how integrated your child is in the school. Will they be in a self-contained classroom for the entire day? Will they have some regular/inclusion classes? How you answer these questions and where your comfort level lies will vary.

Some parents and caregivers have no choice in any of these decisions; others may be able to make decisions based on their situation.

There are great schools, motivated students, and potential good friends available everywhere. There are also less-than-ideal schools, unmotivated students, and individuals who are poor friend choices.

One-on-One with a Mom of a Special-Needs Child

Your best bet is to get to know your school, the students, and the environment where your child will be spending his or her time. The better you are informed and the more involved you can be, the more successful your student will be in handling anything that comes their way.

The issue of bullying is a hot topic for typically developing children and especially for children with special needs. I offer two basic ideas to deal with this issue.

First, if at all possible, visit the school often. Show up at different times of day on different days of the week. When possible bring snacks to share with the class or a small token to your child's teachers just to let them know you appreciate all they do for your child. This can even be as simple as a handwritten note.

Visiting unannounced and showing appreciation to the staff will let them know you are paying attention and care about what goes on around your child. Teachers who know that you are attentive and who know that you appreciate all they do will tend to look out for your child. In essence, "the squeaky wheel gets the grease."

Second, this also allows other students to see who you are and that you will be around from time to time. This can be as simple as driving by and observing them on the playground or spending time in the classroom as a teacher's helper. It may require that you use time off, but in the end, it is worth the cost of ensuring your child's welfare when you are away from them at work or otherwise.

Always remember, kindness goes a long way in breaching walls and mending fences. It is better to spend time with your children in their various environments than to just assume they are handling everything on their own.

Becoming involved and being present in your children's lives also applies to one's typically developing children. Depending on the child's age and grade-level, parental involvement can include something as simple as attending open house, carpooling students to sporting or musical events, or volunteering at a concessions booth. Be present in your children's lives. They and others will know you care, and you will learn a lot and receive more than you realize. It's about contributing and giving back. You will make a positive impact on your children, on their friends, and on others.

Question 11
Will my child have "regular" friends?

Whether your child will have "regular" friends may depend on the type and severity of his or her disability. This is mainly due to how much contact your child may or may not have with other children. But, for the most part, your child will have friends. Your special-needs child may even have more friends than your typically developing children. People are often drawn to kids with special needs and tend to pay a lot of attention to them.

My daughter knows everyone in our church, by name, and she receives hugs and attention all around. She plays with the younger kids when they are playing in the church building. She hangs out with the teens when they are standing around talking. She meets and greets people as they enter the building. Essentially, she has more than just peer relationships; she has relationships with people of all ages.

I will be candid here and say that our daughter with Down syndrome does not have a "best friend" as her typically developing siblings have had. She does not invite friends over or go out with buddies to church activities. She has never really had this type of relationship with "peer" friends. However, her love tank spills over with all the love and attention she receives from others and the love she shows to others. In one sense, I think this is a benefit for the teenage years. My typically developing teens tended to be so bogged down in themselves and their friends that they often truly missed out on relationships with adults and with younger children. It has been beautiful to observe this phenomenon transpire with our daughter.

Everyone's situation is different. My daughter has some mental delay; therefore, she does not relate to her peers on the same level. If your child only has a physical disability, his or her situation may present differently.

The point here is that the more you get out with your child and help them show love to others, the more others will be drawn to them and accept them.

One-on-One with a Mom of a Special-Needs Child

Question 12
Will my child live a "normal" childhood?

Do you often wonder if your son or daughter will have a "normal" childhood? The answer is yes, and no. Our special-needs children are, first and foremost, children. They are often more like everyone else than they are different. Most of the time, their differences become a blessing more than a curse.

Your child will grow up in a family and be loved like other children. Exactly how this happens depends on their situation. Some of them will attend school, learn to walk and talk, play and have friends. Others may never leave their house except for doctor/hospital visits, and they may have limited access to others.

Normal is relative. "Normal" in a family with a special-needs child is redefined by what became the new "normal" when that special child joined the family. What each of us individually has experienced in our own childhoods can be vastly different, yet alike in many ways.

Try not to get discouraged when your "normal" may not be your next-door neighbor's "normal." Remember that we all are doing the best we can with where we are and with what we have.

Your new normal will begin when you realize you have begun to accept your child the way they are and when you have begun to accept your situation. Acceptance is a process. The book, *Extraordinary Kids*, by Cheri Fuller and Louise Tucker, offers the following advice (page 38):

Steps to Acceptance

Martha Little, mother of a child with special needs, offers the following steps to acceptance:

Acknowledge that God's hand was on your child or children in the way they were formed before birth, according to His plan.

Admit any areas you resent in the way God made them.

Accept God's design for them. Thank Him for their personalities and the way they are.

Affirm God's purpose in creating them for His glory.

Ally yourself with God in His plans for them.

One-on-One with a Mom of a Special-Needs Child

"Our job is to see our children as God does and to involve ourselves in His plans, not our own," Martha says.

The best advice I can offer: Be thankful. Train yourself to be thankful for anything and everything you have. A grateful heart nurtures a happy heart. Even during the difficult times in life, I have trained myself to thank God for the messes. A grateful, happy heart begins to change my attitude, my demeanor, and my outlook, which then affects those around us, even our children with special needs. The more we help them to be positive, the better they learn to cope with the diverse and changing situations in life.

Try this the next time you feel discouraged: Train yourself to begin thanking God even for the difficult things in life. You will be amazed at the transformation.

Question 13

As a two-parent family, how do we grow in our marriage and not allow the challenges of raising a special-needs child (or caring for a special-needs loved one) to strain our relationship?

Just for the record, this answer is for married couples dealing with special-needs children or loved ones. If you are single, divorced, or getting out of a relationship, please seek out an individual who can be a safe place to talk and get encouragement. It is paramount to have at least one safe person with whom you can vent, share, and help sort out your emotions.

I personally know people who have successfully raised a child with special needs and had no apparent marriage issues; I also know others who have divorced. I want to encourage you that dealing with special needs can, in fact, strengthen your marriage. Every marriage requires work and effort by both partners; however, caring for an individual with special needs increases stress in a relationship.

I have three words of spousal advice for this topic: Pray, communicate, and be intimate with your spouse. These suggestions may seem odd and rather blunt, but let me explain.

One-on-One with a Mom of a Special-Needs Child

All marriages can benefit from prayer. Pray for wisdom in your marriage, pray for God's blessing in your marriage, pray for problem areas and all the difficult things in life, and pray for your spouse. God asks us to bring everything to Him, at any time, in prayer. He will listen, He will act, and He will help. If you are not regularly doing this, you are simply missing out on one of God's greatest blessings. I highly recommend praying for every aspect in your life and in your marriage.

I will add that some marriages have issues besides dealing with special-needs children. Prayer can still help. God cares. If you or your child are in a dangerous situation, please seek help, from both God and organizations or the authorities.

The next key is communication. (This will be covered in more detail later.) Marriages are challenging enough at times with the busyness of life. Talking and working through life's struggles with your spouse is paramount, and the added stress of caring for someone with special needs can be daunting and overwhelming. Spending time simply talking and listening can make all the difference. Ask your spouse to join with you in resolving problems, issues, and just general day-to-day caregiving.

Date nights and simply spending quality time together (without the children) is beyond important. You do not have to spend a lot, or any money for that matter. Just taking time away enjoying each other's company can do the trick. However, when life gets in the way and difficult things come up—or illness or simply busy schedules—time together can fall by the wayside. But, persist; it will be worth it in the end.

Counseling can always be a boost to your marriage—even if you feel you have no apparent or no major issues. Couples' retreats or conferences not only create a time to get away without the children, but they are designed to improve communication and increase intimacy between you and your spouse. Just know that it is always okay to seek help.

This last one is essential: Intimacy. Yes, I said sexual intimacy. You may research the topic on your own, but data confirms that the more intimacy in your marriage, the better your marriage will be. Let us be realistic here. Making love really does not require a major amount of time, usually around 30 minutes. Am I right? So, no excuses. You will be in bed at some point for at least a few hours, so make the most of some of that time to better your marriage.

I cannot stress this one enough. Making love to your spouse is one of THE most important ways to work on your marriage. If you need more reasons, here are a few good ones: It is a good cardio exercise and burns many calories, it helps your immune system, and it is an energy booster. The reasons for sexual intimacy with your spouse go on and on.

Maybe you do not believe me or you have decided to read no further. However, stick with me. Maybe you are a woman who just does not like sexual intimacy. I promise that if you get some new lingerie, clean your bedroom, put clean sheets on the bed, even get a new comforter and pillows, and add some candles and music in the room for ambience, you will find yourself enjoying personal time with your spouse.

Sexual intimacy with your spouse cannot be just a one-time thing. It certainly does not have to be every night or set on a calendar, but intimacy should be a regular occurrence. Remember, it does not require much time, but, enjoy each other frequently enough to enhance your relationship for BOTH of you. Intimate time alone with your spouse can be tricky to work in when children are in the house, and especially when teens are in the house since they have a later bedtime. Find the time. Make time. Be spontaneous and creative. Mornings, lunch breaks, and afternoons may also work well depending on the day.

You will be amazed at how your relationship blossoms when you make intimate time together an important aspect of your marriage. At some point, you fell in love with your spouse; it can happen all over again.

Question 14
I feel overwhelmed. What can I do to help myself?

There will be moments and even days when you feel overwhelmed, especially during times of sickness and stress. It is just part of your new normal. One of my all-time favorite quotes is, "This, too, shall pass." If today is difficult, usually tomorrow will be better, or at least a future tomorrow will be better. Praying and whispering Jesus' name strengthens me when life seems relentless.

Remember, all these things are new for you. You will eventually settle into a new normal for you and your family. Things will come up which you never even dreamed would happen. For instance, I used to play with dolls when I was little and pretend I was in church with my husband and sweet little family in the pews. I would lovingly attend to my children and occasionally lean over to my husband and whisper something to him. It was a beautiful scenario. I never once in my fairytale world dreamed that I would one day lean over to my child in church and say, "Get your tongue out of your nose." Trust me; this has happened more than once, during church services. I also never imagined that my daughter would walk down the aisle swinging her bra in her hand! At the moment when I saw her, I had no idea where she had actually removed the bra. Oh, the joy!

These are funny now, but there have been other times when serious, hurtful, or just plain difficult things have occurred, and we were at a loss as to what to do. But, through it all, we learned to work together and take one thing and one day at a time and do the best we could with where we were and with what we had.

Good communication with your spouse comes into play at this point. If you are single, I recommend that you find one or two people whom you can trust and who are your "safe place" to vent your anger and frustrations. Difficult things will happen. You will become frustrated and get angry, and trust me when I say these are all quite normal. Remember, God is just a prayer away, and He can take whatever you give Him or toss His way. He is simply waiting for you to come to Him, to ask and give Him the opportunity to help.

Question 15
Will I ever have "me time" when I have a special-needs child?

As the mother of a special-needs child, "me time" may be more elusive, but it is doable. One of the things I have learned over the last 17 years has been that "me time" really is not a thing. Now, stay with me here. I do have an important note on this concept.

First, Jesus kind of had "me time", although, in reality, it truly was not just Him. He was always with His Father and the Spirit. They ARE one. But, He did go off by Himself to be with Them. He would go and spend all night with Them or just find a secluded place to simply be with Them in prayer. The fact that Jesus needed time with His Father demonstrates the importance of prayer and the necessity of our making time to be with our heavenly Father.

Other than times to be with God, Jesus was serving. It is called self-sacrifice, and it is not a bad thing.

The more often that I attempted to get "me time", usually, the more frustrated I would become with how unsatisfying that time away from others, from my family, and from my special-needs child was in reality. My "me time" did not always work out the way I wanted, or the time was elusive. I learned that I became dissatisfied with my "normal" situation, and I longed to be free of the whole situation. However, when I learned to relax in my service and to be grateful and thankful for it, I became better able to handle the daily habit and routine of giving myself to others. Eventually, I found joy in my own "new normal."

This did not happen all at once. At first, I fought and screamed, a lot, and I simply demanded more time for myself. But, even when I managed to snag some "me time", it was never enough.

Now, do I just go about happily serving today and never get "me time"? Well, no and yes. It is a little complicated, and it actually has more to do with my attitude than my "me time".

You see, my normal is not like everyone else's normal. I hear people say things about what they like to do in their off time. People talk about activities like hiking, biking, shopping, walking, or any number of things which they enjoy doing. I do some of these things occasionally, if I have a sitter, or sometimes, I take my daughter along for a few of these activities, but it just isn't the same. I do not have the freedom to just drop something and go do what I want to do, ever. I must always consider my daughter at some point.

Please realize that I have come to terms with this, and for the most part, it is not an issue anymore. This is just my normal and my family's normal and how we roll. At the same time, my husband and I have an understanding. If there is something I would really like to do "by myself", we are usually able to work it out. My mantra these days is "Camille is my shadow." We are salt and pepper, peanut butter and jelly, or hand-and-glove. We just go together.

Am I always okay with this arrangement? It is my life, my normal, and it has become second nature and a habit. So, most of the time, yes, I am okay with Camille's being my shadow. However, sometimes, of course, I would appreciate more freedom. But, it works for us, and we love each other. Camille and I have our own jokes and secret handshakes, and we get along nicely for the most part. It is give-and-take with us, as it should be.

Everyone's situation is different. Everyone has a breaking point. Pay attention to your thoughts and feelings, and when you need time away, do what it takes to take a break. It may not always be on your terms and on your own time, but it will and can happen.

Question 16
Are there groups and/or support groups available for individuals who have situations like mine?

Absolutely! It may take a little digging on your part, but most of the time you can find support groups. I have friends in the homeschool community who would be willing to drive an hour or more from home for their children to take part in some activity. So, depending on where you live, you may need to consider traveling a little to find groups with children like yours or to find caregiver support groups.

You may also discover conventions related to your child's disability. A good place to start is on the internet. Just search key words relating to your child's or individual's disability. Facebook groups abound with all kinds of helpful blogs. It can be daunting at times, but hang in there, and keep searching until you find the right group or groups that fit your needs.

It takes courage to put yourself out there. It also requires courage to admit you need some assistance. It will take courage to meet new people. Again, ask God for direction and wisdom in the process, and realize that not every group is going to be a good fit for your or your child. You know what you need. Be willing to say, "Yes" to what you need and "No" to what is not helpful. Remember, nothing is forever. What might be helpful today may not be as beneficial in the future.

Question 17
I have a special-needs daughter. How do I teach her about her period?

Teaching a special-needs daughter how to take care of her own menstruation cycles can be challenging. To answer this question honestly and fairly, I should tell you a funny story. (Well, it was not so amusing at the time!)

Our daughter with Down syndrome is 17 years old now, and she knows what to do when she starts her period. (At least she knows what to do when she notices evidence on her chair, underwear, bed, or wherever she might be!) Now that she sees what is happening, she will get another pair of underwear and pants, go to the bathroom and take all the soiled things off, put them in the hamper, and call for me to come help her. But, it hasn't always been this easy—not in the least.

My special-needs daughter began menstruating rather early (she was around 10 or 11 years old), and I was not prepared. I had thought about it, but I had not bought anything for the occasion, nor had I decided on a plan of how to proceed.

The first time it happened, she called for me in the bathroom and just said, "Mom, it's red!" Fortunately, my oldest daughter and I had some sanitary napkins to spare, so I put one in place for her. The most-difficult part was teaching her to just keep it in on. She would go to the bathroom and take it off, and then she would go back to her bedroom. It was a constant battle trying to teach her to keep it on at first. Then, when her period was over, she did not easily realize that she did not need to wear the sanitary napkins for a few weeks.

Shortly after my special-needs daughter started her periods, both of my daughters and I went to an out-of-town ladies' retreat. This proved in one way to be good training for her because I was with her every time she needed to go to the bathroom.

On the way home, I was driving down the interstate doing about 75 mph, when all-of-a-sudden, a dirty pad came flying from the backseat into the front of the car. (Yes, you read that correctly, a dirty, used pad!) My oldest daughter was in the passenger seat and screamed. I yelled for her to pick it up off the floor, to which she replied, "No way!" I had to lean over and pick it up. We found an old tissue and wrapped it up and stopped at the next exit to put a new pad on my daughter! This happened all to the

One-on-One with a Mom of a Special-Needs Child

delight of my daughter with Down syndrome who had successfully removed said pad from her pants and gotten rid of the thing!

Hopefully, your experience will not be as dramatic. However, for some children, it just takes a lot of practice and their paying attention to what is going on with their bodies and in learning how to properly take care of themselves. It also requires an incredible amount of patience and willingness to clean and wash garments.

I hereby give you permission to throw away any garments, bedding, or other items rather than having to wash and rinse them out!

Sometimes, life is just too short to have to deal with such dirty things!

My daughter has a mental delay, so our issues stem mostly from her inability to communicate and understand certain concepts. But, she pretty much knows what to do now, which is quite helpful. Train your special-needs child to do whatever is easiest for you in various situations. I want to stress here that when training them, be very careful and make sure they learn to do exactly what they need to do, the way you want them to do it. My daughter is extremely rigid in how she does things, so consistently practice what you want them to be able to do.

For those of you who have a daughter who may need physical assistance, devise a plan ahead of time to help her be as discreet as possible. You won't get it right the first time. But, with a solid plan and lots of practice and patience, your special-needs child will learn and succeed.

Question 18
How do I teach my special-needs child about sexuality?

Dealing with the topic of sex with a special-needs child has unique challenges. My daughter with Down syndrome does not process information and understand male-female relationships in the same way as other typically developing teenagers.

Okay, this is a sensitive topic, and I have no real proven way to help you. But, I will say that currently it is just not an issue with my daughter. The most-important thing I have done so far is to know where she is and with whom she is at all times. This can be difficult, but it works for us.

I have had talks at church with our teens about our daughter and how to help her in her relationships with others. She loves men, in general, and she likes their attention. She has a great dad, and she gets lots of appropriate love from him. But, I have had to tell the teen boys at church to not allow her to sit on their laps once she got older. It was cute when she was little, but around the time a young lady approaches her preteens, this behavior can cause unnecessary issues.

There may be a day in the future when she "likes a boy"—maybe someone who is like her. But, for now, our daughter is just a happy young lady who has all kinds of friends and loved ones who love and care for her.

I do know that several organizations, such as the National Down Syndrome affiliates, have documents and information relating to this very issue. Organizations dealing with autism, cerebral palsy, and many others have information online. Any reputable counselor should be able to direct you for help with your specific situation.

I caution you as a parent to teach and train your child moral codes of acceptable behavior. If your child is acting out in inappropriate ways, please get help, for their sakes and for yours. It is way more harmful to ignore the problem than to find a solution. Be mindful of TV shows, movies, internet access, phone access, and any place where they might be exposed to something harmful. It is way better to deal with it beforehand than afterward. Remember, there is always hope, and help is available. Just be willing to acknowledge and discuss any problem areas and seek assistance.

Question 19
I am a caregiver to an aging, special-needs individual. How do I help this person maintain his or her dignity?

This is, perhaps, one of the most-difficult types of caregiving. It is painful to watch a parent or loved one age and deal with dementia and/or physical, mental, and/or emotional issues.

My mom began showing signs of dementia around the age of 69, and she passed away about six years later. My father-in-law found a small tumor which ended up being lung cancer, and he died a few short years later. Within a four-year period, my mother-in-law had back surgery, cancer, and a dislocated hip from a fall, and thereafter, she passed away. My father, who had otherwise been healthy, died quite unexpectedly from complications from surgery.

When caring for an aging loved one, it is important to help them maintain as much dignity, respect, honor, and love as possible. Suffering is difficult; watching someone you love suffer is often painful. Being a caregiver in these situations can be draining, especially the longer your caregiving duties are required. It is helpful if others can share responsibility in taking care of an aged parent or loved one. That lessens the burden for any one person.

When your loved one has the ability to comprehend their situation, simply help that individual communicate their thoughts, feelings, and wishes. Make sure they are part of decisions and discussions regarding their care. Help them be realistic about their needs and what you can handle as a caregiver. Open, honest discussion is paramount in helping them maintain their dignity.

When your loved one does not have the mental ability to understand his or her situation due to accidents, trauma, dementia, Alzheimer's, or other situations, it will be up to you and your family to make appropriate decisions.

As your parents age, I recommend obtaining power of attorney, while they have all their faculties. Everyone's situation is different and unique. Another important option is to have them write out their wishes in a Living Will. This way you know ahead of time what they desire in their later years.

These are all difficult things to do, but they are necessary to best help the individuals navigate their later years with as much dignity as possible.

Question 20
How do I adequately care for and assist an aging parent and/or an elderly loved one?

Caring for and assisting an elderly individual or loved one brings its own unique challenges. Again, first go to God in prayer, and ask Him for wisdom. If you do not have the resources, ask God to provide what is needed.

Obtain help making decisions. Social workers, organizations, and all kinds of specialized help are available. Research and discover what works best for the individual and for you as a caregiver.

Caring for the elderly is much different from caring for a young person with a disability. Typically, your goal with an older individual is to keep them as active as possible for as long as feasible. Understand that they are spiraling down in life rather than just beginning. This sounds logical, but we often have unrealistic expectations.

Honor their wishes, but realize that some wishes cannot be kept. I know elderly people who made their loved ones promise to not place them in a nursing home or assisted living of any kind. This is just not healthy or realistic. Sometimes, it is necessary to get outside help or to have someone cared for in a facility when you just cannot physically or mentally do it yourself. Know your limitations. Take care of yourself first so that you can take care of others, including your immediate family.

Some decisions in life are particularly difficult. Be willing to talk about your feelings, and if your elderly loved one or individual is able, talk to them about their feelings. Share your situation with others, and be open, honest, and straightforward with the struggles with which you are dealing. Talking with someone can help clarify decisions that must be made. There are professionals who specialize in helping families make informed decisions regarding the elderly and disabilities. The more you internalize and deny your feelings, the harder it is on you all the way around.

Nursing homes often have a bad reputation. They are, for the most part, understaffed and undertrained. But, the purpose of a nursing home is to allow someone to live and die with dignity. Most of us probably hope to die peacefully and quietly in our sleep; however, the reality is that most of us will need care as we get older.

Think how you want to be treated, and act accordingly with your loved one to the best of your ability. You are their advocate. Even if they are unwilling or unable to admit it, they need your help at times.

PRACTICAL WAYS TO HELP OTHERS MAINTAIN THEIR DIGNITY:

1. Keeping your loved one as safe as possible. This should be your top priority. Just like for your children, take steps to help prevent the elderly from injuring or hurting themselves or someone else. For some aging individuals, daily activities such as taking a shower or bath, walking outside in bad weather, driving, cooking, shopping, and even answering the door can pose serious problems. When you see discrepancies in any of these areas, pay attention and take precautions.

   Some agencies will conduct a driving test for your loved one. Keep in mind, that should your loved one be involved in an accident, you certainly do not want them to hurt themselves, but you absolutely do not want them potentially hurting someone else.

   Taking away their keys may be a difficult, yet necessary decision. You may even have to disconnect something on the car to keep it from starting. But, do whatever it takes if you truly believe your aging loved one does not have the ability to drive safely.

2. Make sure your aging loved one is dressing appropriately. Once you notice unusual behavior, you may need to make decisions for their care. Sometimes they will overdress or underdress. Dressing inappropriately can not only be immodest, but if they are not dressed for the weather or climate, they could injure themselves or become ill.

3. Pay attention to their hygiene. Are they brushing their teeth, washing their hair, shaving, bathing, and toileting, etc.? Help them stay clean and well groomed.

4. Make sure they are eating as healthy as possible. This can be difficult, but one way is to check their fridge and cabinets. Periodically, throw away any old and outdated food.

5. Allow your loved one to respond and answer questions and inquiries for themselves as long as possible. You may sometimes need to give them cues, words, or assistance, but at least let them attempt to respond. Their mind may be perfectly

intact; however, sometimes words and speech do not come easily to some aging individuals.

Pay attention to any discrepancies in these areas since they can be red flags that your aging loved one needs more attentive care. Some of them can be quite stubborn, so help maintain their dignity, but realize that their safety takes priority.

Your aging loved one may just need some extra care temporarily or they may need longterm care. With their permission—and while they are of sound mind—obtain their power of attorney for them and for their healthcare. Know where their important papers are located, and ask them to allow your name (or another trusted individual) to be added onto their bank accounts. This will enable you to assist them with their finances—paying bills and purchasing necessities for them. However, ask permission before proceeding with the above tasks. Do not presume that they will allow access or provide you with these things.

There are horrible people out there who take advantage of their loved ones. Do what you can to take care and honor your aging loved ones.

Six Key Strategies for Victorious Caregiving

Key Strategy #1: Prayer

Take your child or other loved one straight to the throne of God. Start praying today, and pray daily. Ask God to show you how to work with your loved one and that ask that He help both of you be all He wants you to be. Ask for wisdom and grace to face each new day.

If you do not have a relationship with God, please seek Him out. Find a friend who has a strong faith, go to church, read the Bible, and/or simply pray from your heart for Him to guide you in this special journey. I promise that you will not be disappointed.

Why pray, and why prayer? It is our lifeline to God. Have you ever thought much about God's being a triune God—God the Father, God the Son, and God the Holy Spirit? Think about this for a minute: They are in a relationship. They are not one self-serve Being. It is, has been, and always will be all about relationship with God. He longs for us to be in a relationship with Him. This is the whole reason God made us and came down to Earth through Jesus: He desires to be with us.

God gave Adam a wife. God gave us the temple so we would have a place to worship Him together. God gave Himself in Jesus to come and be with us. God gave us His Word to show us the way. God gave us the Holy Spirit to live in us and to be part of our lives. He wants to be involved in our lives and for us to desire a relationship with Him. God provided the concept of family and friendship so that we might be in relationships with each other, as well.

God literally stands at the door of our hearts and knocks.

Revelation 3:20 (The Message) says, "Here I am! I stand at the door and knock. If anyone hears my voice and opens the door, I will come in and eat with him, and he with Me."

Even if you don't really know how to pray, God has that covered, too. The disciples once asked Jesus to teach them how to pray,

He said to them, "When you pray, say:

> 'Father,
> Hallowed be your name,
> Your kingdom come,
>
> Give us each day our daily bread.
> Forgive us our sins,
> For we also forgive everyone who sins against us.
> And lead us not into temptation.'" Luke 11:2-4 (NIV)

Jesus' prayer covers our praise for God and who He is, and Jesus asks God to meet our most basic needs, especially our spiritual needs in and for God.

Back in Matthew 6:5-8 (NIV), Jesus teaches them further about prayer, "And when you pray . . . go into your room, close the door and pray to your Father, who is unseen. Then your Father who sees what is done in secret, will reward you . . . for your Father knows what you need before you ask Him."

One-on-One with a Mom of a Special-Needs Child

Our prayers are personal and private. There is no need for pomp and circumstance or for posturing. All that is necessary is an open, willing, and humble heart.

Paul tells us to take everything to God in prayer.

"Do not be anxious about anything, but in everything, by prayer and petition, with thanksgiving, present your requests to God. And the peace of God, which transcends all understanding, will guard your hearts and your minds in Christ Jesus." Philippians 4:6-7 (NIV)

We pray, we petition, we thank, and we present. We receive peace, understanding, and protection for our anxious minds.

What all this calls for is a daily, personal, and intimate relationship with God. Talking with God in prayer is the best way to cultivate your relationship with Him.

Prayer is also listening. Remember, it is a relationship, not a one-sided action on our part. God longs to speak to us. Part of our daily, personal, and intimate relationship is to be in the Word, where we learn and listen to what God tells us.

I can honestly say that I have never heard an audible voice from God, but I can say that I have heard Him speaking to me in other ways. I "hear" God in a gentle nudge to do something, in a thought or thought process, or when someone tells me something I needed to hear, etc.

So, pray anytime, and pray all the time. Take everything to God. He is standing at the door waiting for you to share with Him and talk with Him.

Ever wonder what happens to all your prayers? Are they just words you speak and then they disappear? Does God forget about the things we bring before Him?

Revelation 5:6-8 (NIV) tells us clearly about the importance of our prayers to God. This is a direct throne-room scene: "Then I saw a Lamb . . . the four living creatures and the twenty-four elders fell down before the Lamb. Each one had a harp and they were holding golden bowls full of incense, which are the prayers of the saints."

Described in the Bible many times as a pleasing aroma, our prayers are like bowls of incense before God.

That is pretty awesome! God stands and knocks at the door of our hearts, He comes and teaches us how to pray, and He keeps these prayers close to Him as a pleasing aroma right at His throne.

Know that your prayers can be thought, whispered, said, shouted, and even screamed before God 24/7. If you ever worry about your prayers being angry prayers or vengeful prayers, read through the Psalms. David had some harsh words for God. God can take it. He is more interested in your relationship and in your heart than He is about what you say.

If you are angry, tell God. If you are hurt, take it to Him. If you are mad at Him, let Him know. Spill it all out at the foot of the cross. God hears it all anyway, so you may as well just take it to the One with whom you are angry. God allowed David, and even Job to speak freely with Him.

The more you practice talking to God in a closed room by yourself, the more comfortable you will be with Him. He knows about your struggles, and He cares, even about the difficult things. God allows us the chance to come before Him with anything at any time, day or night. He never rests nor sleeps.

Pray, petition, thank, and present. Receive peace, understanding, and protection for your anxious minds.

Prayer is an important key strategy for victorious caregiving. God sees, He longs for a relationship with us, He cares, and He wants us to rely on Him for everything.

Pray!

Key Strategy #2: Asking for Help

This is a tough one. As mothers, most of us do not often ask for help. Moms and caregivers tend to be control freaks. Let me explain.

> Me: Knock, knock!
> You: Who's there?
> Me: Control Freak.
> Me (butting in to answer): Control Freak who?

Get it? It can be difficult to let someone do something that we know (or think we know) we can do better, or at least think we can. Some of us would run ourselves ragged and into the ground before asking anyone for help. Sometimes it is way easier to do something ourselves rather than explain how it needs to be done.

One-on-One with a Mom of a Special-Needs Child

So, how do you ask for help and sincerely accept it?

Start with the little things. Ask someone to carry something for you. Most people do not feel comfortable doing things for your child or loved one, so ask them to do something for you. Make a list of simple tasks that just about anyone could do.

SIMPLE TASKS FOR OTHERS TO DO FOR YOU:

1. Give you a hug and a smile every time they see you.

2. Send an encouraging text message to you.

3. Save a convenient seat for you in a public space.

4. Invite you to go out for coffee or offer to bring coffee to you at your home.

5. Meet you at the car at church and help you carry something into the building.

6. Sit by, stand next to, and/or watch your child while you go to the restroom.

These are all ways to learn to ask for help. As you practice asking others to assist you with these tasks, you will become more comfortable requesting bigger things in the future. It is okay to ask for help now and then. You will need to learn this skill because at times, you will really need assistance.

There are two basic components to this strategy. The first component includes things you can do to make your life easier; the second component consists of what to avoid so that your life will run more smoothly.

Component 1: How do I Ask for Help?

When you are overwhelmed, how do you ask for help? Where do you even start? What is the first thing I am going to tell you to do? Yes, pray! Take everything to God, every day.

This one strategy of asking for assistance is the most difficult by far. In our control-freak mother/father/caregiving mode, we think we are the superwoman of all superwomen or superman of all supermen, whichever the case may be. We think, "I do not need help. I do not need your sympathy. I can do it all. I can bring home the bacon and fry it up in a pan, thank you very much!"

But, if you could only see the inside. We are tired, exhausted, and spent beyond measure. On top of everything, most of us are involved with various ministries outside the home. We teach Sunday school, we take food to others, and we offer to do things for which we need the assistance of others. We just keep piling it on and on.

We wonder why we are so tired and achy all the time. We wonder why we snap at our families, but show loving grace to others. We are a pretty pathetic lot. Notice that I am including myself and saying "we".

Consider the following ideas and actions to motivate yourself to ask and to allow others to assist you: Praying for you, your family, and your special-needs child or individual, make casseroles/prepare meals, loan books for you to read or suggest library books to check out, run errands, do laundry, assist with housecleaning, etc. All of the above are helpful to parents and caregivers.

WAYS TO ALLOW AND ASK FOR HELP:

1. Make a list of things people could do for you. This list might include providing needed supplies, sitting with or for your loved one, or any of the above-listed tasks. Keep a handy mental in your mind or physical list on paper or on your phone to mention to someone who is offering help. Contact these individuals, and ask them for a specific favor.

2. Ask your family to contribute and do their part. Your spouse and children are often capable of doing more than you realize. Make a list of tasks or areas that need attention, and then divvy them out accordingly.

3. Pray and ask God for wisdom and assistance. But, just because you pray, does not mean that God is going to swoop in and save the day. Sometimes, in His wisdom and His perfect timing, He may need you to carry on and stay the course. He will help you always, just not always as you wish.

4. If your loved one is on a prayer list at your church, ask that your name be included as the caregiver. We tend to forget about our caregivers. Do not be embarrassed or ashamed to do this.

Ask for wisdom, mercy, and love in your caregiving responsibilities.

5. Realize that help comes in many different forms—physical, mental, emotional, and spiritual. Maybe you just need a listening ear, maybe you need help with a household task, maybe you need some spiritual guidance, or maybe you just need a break. These are all legitimate, basic needs.

6. Finally, learn to appreciate random acts of kindness. When you feel lonely and down, think of the top three things you wish someone would do for you. If you are physically able, do them for someone else. It does not have to require money or even much time, but just do something for someone else. Mail a card, text encouraging words to a friend, or pray for someone and let them know you are praying. It is even more fun when you can do these anonymously!

Asking for help is difficult. Letting someone help you can be humbling. Knowing your limits and admitting them is insightful. But, with God's help and wisdom, you can move forward victoriously in your caregiving.

Component 2: Rest

The one thing we often need the most is rest. But, as caregivers, allowing ourselves to rest can be difficult. We just keep going and going, adding to our schedules and trying to help our family, as well as others around us. We must not stop. We must carry on. We must make sure each of our children are involved in everything, and we must keep up with all the latest ministries and our own passions and desires.

At times in my past, God has forced me to slow down and made me do nothing except take care of my family. It is by far the hardest place to be, but God knows we need these times. Over the years, I have relaxed and become less of a people pleaser, and I rather enjoy saying no and sitting things out.

Slow down, and consider the following:

- As a wife, mother, and caregiver, you are primarily responsible for your own family. Your husband is top priority, and your children come second. Yes, you read that correctly. Your relationship with your spouse is number one. If you want a healthy marriage and a happy home, take care of your husband physically, mentally, spiritually, and sexually. You want your spouse there when your children grow up and leave home, even if your special-needs child or loved one may still be home a bit longer. Your spouse should be your best friend. It is never too late to start working on this part of your relationship.

- Your children come second. This is hard for some people to read and comprehend. Your children do not have to be involved in every outside activity. For a few years, we limited our children's sports activities to one per season. Our family schedule was still chaotic, but it was more manageable. There were also a couple of years during which our kids did not participate in anything except church activities.

- There will be seasons when your typically developing children will take a second seat to your child or loved one with the disability. This is perfectly okay. It is a lesson they need to learn: Life is not always about us and what we want. Sometimes, life requires give and take; sometimes it calls for self-sacrifice. Remember, these are seasons, not the whole of life. For your children, taking one year off doing nothing except going to school and coming home to your family is acceptable.

You can learn to make sweet memories by just paying attention to and getting to know each of your kids.

- Moms, your job is to be a mom. Regardless of whether you work outside the home or if you stay at home as a caregiver, your number-one job is to take care of your family. When you have preschool- and school-aged children, especially, learn to say no to many things outside of your work and home. Be selective about how you spend your time and energy. This does not mean that you cannot pursue anything you love to do, but your family should take priority over outside activities—even church and ministry activities. Consider your family your ministry during this time. Unless you can do something as a family, say no. I promise there will be seasons where you can concentrate on your hobbies, ministries, and talents.

As a superhero-caregiver mom, you may find this difficult to hear. But, if you continue to try and "do it all," the busyness will catch up with you and wear you down.

One-on-One with a Mom of a Special-Needs Child

When my third child was born with Down syndrome in May 2001, my husband had minor back surgery that same summer. Then that fall, I started homeschooling our oldest daughter, and we became active in a homeschool co-op. Two years later, my husband had major back surgery. At that time, I was a Brownie troop leader, I helped with several co-op classes, both of my older children began playing in a few different sports, and my youngest daughter was going to therapy multiple times a week. I did these things and took my children to their various activities all while homeschooling. I was a wreck, mentally, physically, and spiritually. I was a pathetic and tired wife, a grumpy and agitated mom, and a horrible homeschool teacher. Something had to give.

I had to learn the hard way that I just could not do it all. We prayerfully decided to limit our kids' activities and do this one year at a time. I had to bow out of some ministry stuff and just learn to say no to things other than those which pertained to my home and my homeschooling. It was the hardest and best decision we could have ever made.

I could never have attempted to write a book, pursue a ministry, do a blog, or do anything else besides being a wife, mom, and caregiver, during that time in my life.

But, guess what? My older children are grown and out of the house now, and I can do so much more now than I ever thought possible. It took a while, but my family was way better off to have all of me, rather than just part of me.

Key Strategy #3: Communication

My seventh-grade math teacher had a saying every time someone complained about something's not being fair. He would always respond with, "Fair comes in September." Over the years, I have found myself repeating this phrase to myself and my children. Life just isn't always fair.

Communication is the key which allows everyone to learn to deal with the unfairness in life. In its simplest form, communication is give-and-take with information, where the give-and-take is equally important.

Learning how to communicate within a special-needs family helps everyone get through the difficult moments, days, weeks, months, and oftentimes, years. Families dealing with special needs of any kind have a unique lifestyle. Each family member learns, whether for the good or for the bad, that life is not about

One-on-One with a Mom of a Special-Needs Child

them. I have learned a lot along the way as the mom of a special-needs daughter.

I am a big believer in telling people like it is. There may be times when wisdom suggests that withholding information is necessary; however, everyone needs to learn to deal with life as it happens.

When it comes to dealing with special needs within a family, communication is paramount for the health and wellbeing of each family member. Talk about everything—the good, the bad, and the ugly. Talk about your feelings, your concerns, your dreams, and your ideas. Allow everyone in the family the chance to do the same.

The primary caregiver needs a safe, trustworthy person to whom he or she can vent and share thoughts and feelings. Whether your confidante is your spouse, a trusted friend, a family member, or even a counselor, make sure you have someone with whom you can confide and who will support you. This individual should understand that their role is not to fix everything, but to allow you to share your feelings in confidence. A word of caution here: If you are married and your spouse is not your confidante, be extremely careful whom you choose as your confidante. As I have said before, your spouse is your number-one priority; guard this relationship with your life.

One important factor to remember is to include your entire immediate family. Everyone who lives in the house with the special-needs individual must be included and/or taken into consideration when making decisions, plans, etc. These are the only people who truly matter. NO ONE ELSE MATTERS! It is no one else's business how you manage your home. Of course, do everything in a godly way. Why is this important? Life is difficult enough without hearing the unsolicited opinions and advice of those who do not live within your household. I realize that with some families, this can be quite tricky. But, to the best of your ability, keep your family business as private as possible.

Think of your family as a team. To compete in the game of life, everyone needs to feel important to the team. Each member in the immediate family should be amenable or at least mostly on board with how you are going to move forward as you learn to deal with your own family's unique situation with disability.

It is going to affect each person differently. Siblings must learn to adjust to seasons of therapies or illnesses where they may not get to do the things they prefer. Finances may become tighter as more resources are needed to care for the person with the disability. Some members of the family may also be less tolerant of the disabled child or individual. When this occurs, it may also result in problems with individuals outside the immediate family.

For a successful family life, communication and teamwork is crucial. Learn to communicate with each family member and create an environment conducive to favorable and active participation with how things will flow at any given time. It is important to include and talk with every family member. Even your youngest children understand more than you realize.

If someone in the family is struggling with a particular issue, encourage them and help them share their feelings. Make sure your home is a safe place for each family member to express their emotions. This does not mean someone can scream and cry for what they want. But, it does mean that they should have the chance to learn how to communicate appropriately.

Allow emotions—joy, sadness, and even anger—to flow freely, but always in an appropriate way and setting. Reassure the individual that God cares, that you care, and that you are there for them. The more you talk about difficult things in life, especially as they occur, the more everyone feels free to talk. It is healthy to share and talk about feelings respectfully instead of internalizing them.

Listening is half of communication. While someone is talking, listen. Truly hear what they are saying. Expect the same in return when you speak. Repeat back what was said to verify that what you heard was what they meant. Ask them to do the same. It takes work and practice, but everyone will appreciate and benefit from knowing that someone is listening and hearing what they are relaying to others.

Lastly, make sure that you and everyone else in the immediate family understands that part of communication is just that—saying something out loud. Most of the time just getting something out of your head and expressed is all that is needed. Not everything needs to be fixed. Extend this courtesy to each family member. Learn to ask others what they expect, and ask others to do the same for you.

One-on-One with a Mom of a Special-Needs Child

The Top Three Tips for Successful Communication in a Home with a Special-Needs Individual

Strategic communication is vital to your overall health and wellbeing as a special-needs caregiver. The following are basic ideas to help you on your journey:

1. Find a confidante with whom to talk, vent, and share ideas. Your spouse, sibling, friend or whomever you choose should be trustworthy and supportive. They need to understand that some days you just need to vent or cry without their wondering if you are unbalanced. A note of caution: If the person to whom you are confiding is not your spouse, be clear about your relationship. Set safe boundaries for yourself and for the other person. You might even consider having two safe people present when you need to vent.

2. Your entire immediate family should be amenable and like-minded with you on this journey. Make a habit of talking about everything with your spouse. Siblings need to be in on the process or at least understand the decisions that you as a caregiver may need to make. I have found it extremely helpful at times to include siblings in

conversations and discussions regarding life with the special-needs individual. Since siblings have a unique perspective that you may not initially understand, they may offer creative ideas and solutions in certain situations. Never feel obligated to share information beyond your safe borders. It is no one's business.

3. Communication with anyone other than your immediate family, spouse, and/or your safe person/confidante is always up to you. However, if other individuals live in your household, it may be helpful and advisable to include them. Their input and interactions with the special-needs individual and with the entire family affect the communication dynamics. They should be apprised and supportive of the family goals regarding the special-needs individual, and they should strive to impact the family and household as a whole in a positive way.

Key Strategy #4: Whispering Jesus' Name

This strategy is closely akin to prayer, simply because it is a prayer. In our day-to-day living, we learn quickly where our faith really lies. We tend to rely on ourselves and our own power, and we learn to pull ourselves up by our own bootstraps. When God puts disability in your life, the tables get turned. You are no longer able to keep up the façade.

Have you ever heard of Gladys Aylward? She was a missionary in China in the early-to-mid-1900s. She left London alone to travel to China and teach the people about Jesus. On her journey there, one horrendous night, deep in communist territory, Gladys came face-to-face with an evil Russian captain. He took her passport, intended to have his way with her, and then sell her to work in a factory.

As the Russian captain came into her room that evening, carrying her passport, Gladys was terrified! She yelled at him, "You can't touch me. You can't touch me. God will protect me!" Laughing at her plight, he reared back to punch her in the face, but she kept yelling the same words over and over. As he began to swing his arm toward her, his hand stopped in midair. "Instead, as if guided by some invisible force, he turned around, opened the door, and walked out." (Page 60)

Gladys managed to get away from him and from the Russians. She boarded a Japanese freighter bound for China. She knew there was power in God's name and in Jesus' name. Boy, was there ever power!

This is going to sound pathetic next to Gladys' story, but I whisper Jesus' name when I am sorting out laundry. I distinctly remember folding clothes one day. It had been a rather difficult day, and I was at the end of my rope. The more I tried to fold clothes the more frustrated I got. Why? Every item of clothing belonging to my daughter with Down syndrome was turned inside out. Are you kidding me? Seriously! Some would say, "Just put them back in her drawer that way, and she will turn the clothes right side out herself."

Well, for crying out loud! She has Down syndrome, you know. She might do this one time out of ten, but the other nine times, everything would be inside out.

During this time, I had been reading a new devotional book by Sarah Young, called *Jesus Calling*. She kept reminding the reader to call on Jesus' name and bring him near in your mind. I sat there with the laundry and just started saying, "Jesus, Jesus, Jesus", over and over. You know what? I calmed down. It really worked. I was no longer frustrated. I continued to fold and kept saying his name every time I came to something that irritated me. Wow! Something so simple really helped.

One-on-One with a Mom of a Special-Needs Child

Jesus is right there with us at all the time. Knowing and trusting Jesus' constant presence makes all the difference in my mind, my heart, my moments, and my day. Calling on Jesus' name centers our minds on Him and where He is with us at that moment in time. It helps us develop a daily, personal, intimate relationship with Him.

I used to sing a song to my children when they were little that demonstrates this idea perfectly. The song is, "There's Something About That Name":

> *Jesus, Jesus, Jesus;*
> *There's just something about that name.*
> *Master, Savior, Jesus,*
> *Like the fragrance after the rain;*
> *Jesus, Jesus, Jesus,*
> *Let all Heaven and earth proclaim;*
> *Kings and kingdoms will all pass away,*
> *But there's something about that name.*

This song by Bill and Gloria Gaither is a sweet and gentle reminder of who Jesus is in our lives. Learn it, sing it over your children, but most of all, sing it over your own heart.

Know Jesus. Call on His name. There is power in the name of Jesus.

On the challenging days, when disability is just difficult, and you don't think you can carry on much longer, call on Jesus and bring Him near. He will help you, He will give you peace, He will give you rest, and He will be right there with you in your moment of need.

John 20:30 & 31 (NIV) reminds us just what life is really all about. (Emphasis mine.)

"Jesus performed many other signs in the presence of his disciples, which are not recorded in this book. But these are written that

> You may believe that Jesus is the Messiah,
> the Son of God,
> and that by believing
> you may have life in His name."

If you ever question whether Jesus will come near, read Revelation 3:20,

"Here I am! I stand at the door and knock. If anyone hears my voice and opens the door, I will come in and eat with him, and he with me."

Not only will He come in, He will sit down at your table and stay awhile. That, my friend, is pretty cool.

If Jesus can help a lonely woman in war-torn China in the middle of nowhere, He can certainly help me in my difficult times.

Bringing Jesus' name to the forefront of your mind or in any grave situation is paramount to making it in this life. Whispering or shouting or using Jesus' name in an affirmative way will allow you to bring Him along with you when you need Him. It is empowering, and it is a blessing.

Key Strategy #5: Gratitude and Thankfulness

Call me old and sentimental, but when I think about gratitude, I sometimes think about an old country song, "I Never Promised You a Rose Garden", written by Joe South and recorded by Lynn Anderson. Life is not always rosy, happy, and joyful. As the song says,

> *"I beg your pardon,*
> *I never promised you a rose garden,*
> *Along with the sunshine, there's got to be a little rain sometimes."*

Even Jesus tells us in John 16:33 (NIV),

"I have told you these things, so that in me you may have peace. In this world, you will have trouble. But take heart! I have overcome the world."

The only way I have found to deal with life's struggles and hardships is to learn to thank God for them. Most importantly, be thankful in "the moment" of suffering. It is only then that I can get the attention away from myself and my problem. I can then lay it down and let God do with it as He must.

I also think of another song, a VeggieTales song called, "I Thank God for This Day", by Phil Vischer. My most favorite line is,

"Because a thankful heart is a happy heart."

I could go on and on with thankful songs all day. One of the first things we teach our children is to say, "Thank You" to others when someone does something for them. Appreciation is considered good manners and proper etiquette.

So, what does this have to do with special-needs caregiving?

When life hands you something you were not expecting, for instance, Down syndrome, dementia,

One-on-One with a Mom of a Special-Needs Child

Cerebral Palsy, Epilepsy, Alzheimer's, stroke, Type 1 Diabetes, or an accident leaving your loved one scarred for life, you tend to wonder just what happened to your rose garden.

I'm not talking about bad hair days or hangnails; I'm talking about life-changing events that rock your world. I'm talking financial trouble, job loss, addiction issues, death, and divorce—things you would never wish on another person.

The only way to truly combat these difficult things is to cultivate thankfulness and gratitude in the garden of our hearts. I Thessalonians 5:16-18 (The Message) says,

"Be cheerful no matter what; pray all the time; thank God no matter what happens. This is the way God wants you who belong to Christ Jesus to live."

Let's break this down a bit.

Paul wrote this letter to a group of young, new Christians who were being persecuted. At the end of the letter, he left them with some final instructions.

"Be joyful always." Always? Yes, be joyful always. Joyful is not happy, hoorah, fun, but instead, being joyful is a purposeful, positive attitude in Jesus.

"Pray continually." Continually? Yes, be in constant communication with Jesus, and be mindful of Him in everything you do and encounter. This is like praying without ceasing.

"Give thanks in all circumstances." All circumstances? Yes! Have you ever cleaned up poop from furniture or carpet? Have you watched someone you love slip away day-by-day? Have you tried to push a wheelchair through a door without any help? Have you had to give your child injections just to keep them alive? Has your daughter taken off and thrown a used sanitary pad in the car? Have you had to suction your child's airways in public? I could go on and on.

I don't know about you, but I have not thanked God lately for any of these things. I am slowly learning to attempt this, but it is not always my first reaction.

Give thanks in all circumstances. Yes! All circumstances.

I admit that I have tried this a few times, and it is quite satisfying. My mind changes, my mood changes, and suddenly, I am aware that God is right there with me in "the moment" of something that is difficult. I am forced "to let go and let God" take on the problem.

One-on-One with a Mom of a Special-Needs Child

The most poignant use of thankfulness in the Bible is when Jesus breaks the bread in the first communion right before he offers Himself to die on the cross. In that moment, Jesus is asking us to understand just what He is doing. He asks us to recognize the significance of His offering to us. We need to remember Jesus and thank Him for what He did.

Jesus always shows us the way. He doesn't just tell us, but He goes first and shows us with His own actions how we are to proceed.

He took the bread, broke it, and gave thanks for it, saying, "This is my Body." We are to do the same, literally and figuratively, every time we partake of it.

Jesus took Himself, broke Himself and His will on the cross, gave thanks to God in the process, and He asks us to live our lives in the same way.

So, even during the difficult times, even in learning to give yourself to others in a life of service to God, learn to be grateful and thankful for what He has done for you.

Instead of saying, "I'm blessed," which is hard to say during the difficulties of life, say "I'm grateful."

Key Strategy #6: Self-Sacrifice in Forgoing Activities

This final key strategy has been the hardest for me to write, yet it is one of the most important and vital keys to understand. Stated simply, when dealing with disability, you must learn to be okay sitting things out, or in other words, learn self-sacrifice in forgoing activities.

One of the things I hear the most in the disability arena is that people with disabilities are more like typically developing people than they are different. I really love this because the idea is that disability should not define a person. A disability is merely an extension of who they are. This idea is meant to teach us that people are people. Period. Everyone is important and deserves respect and a chance to succeed.

Learning to be okay with sitting things out and with forgoing plans are difficult issues to deal with in any given situation. It is a lesson that everyone should learn early on in life. However, our society tends to glorify busyness and not hurting anyone's self-esteem. Whether or not you're in a family with a special-needs child or individual, one must learn to be flexible when circumstances arise which necessitate change.

One-on-One with a Mom of a Special-Needs Child

Sitting things out from a caregiver's perspective:

Caring for someone with a disability has its limitations, whether you care for someone physically disabled, mentally disabled, emotionally disabled, or any combination of these disabilities. At times, it is just not feasible to attempt an activity due to issues beyond your control. The reasons for forgoing activities could be as simple as the weather or noise level, or as complicated as illness and friend issues.

Sometimes, you will be stuck and not able to enjoy a given activity, task, appointment, or whatever may arise. You will have to learn to be okay sitting things out, while others go merrily along without a thought as to why you cannot be a part of an activity or event.

At times you may attempt to participate, but for whatever reason you have to leave altogether, or excuse yourselves, or just sit on the sidelines watching everyone else share in the fun or event.

There will also be times when you will not be invited in the first place. This may be a mistake, a slight, intentional (for various or even heartfelt reasons), or an outright rudeness, but for whatever reason, you will not be going.

Other times, your loved one may be invited, but he or she cannot participate. It is difficult watching everyone else while knowing that your loved one is not in any way capable of participating.

Sometimes you will also have to force your loved one's siblings to miss out simply because you just cannot do two things at once, such as care for your loved one and watch the other children or due to when circumstances beyond your control, such as illness, arise.

While it can be difficult for all of your children to miss out on things, in reality, it is just life. Life is not always easy. It is important to learn for ourselves, our loved one with a disability, and our families that we may not do or be able to do everything we want to do in life. Knowing one's limitations at times and sometimes being disappointed by not always participating in activities is vital to developing a positive self-image. But, you can still be happy, joyful, and perfectly okay.

It is difficult to be a momma, daddy, sibling, caregiver, or loved one to someone with a disability. It is also quite challenging to be the one with the disability.

One-on-One with a Mom of a Special-Needs Child

So, what do you do when you have to sit something out or watch your loved one sit something out?

First, you go to God and ask for wisdom on how to deal with this sensitive issue. Read through the gospels, and see how Jesus dealt with people and situations. He was not always liked or invited, and the times He was invited, it was usually a trap to see what He would do. Basically, Jesus loved and reacted in love to those around Him, especially to the downtrodden, the poor, the lonely, the sad, and the sick.

Second, keep praying and asking God to help you and your loved one maneuver your journey with grace. Jesus said we will have troubles in this life, but He also said He was the answer, because He had overcome.

Third, have open conversations with your special-needs loved one (if possible) and your family about what is doable for you and what may not be doable. Teach yourself and your family that it is okay to put someone else before yourself. There will be times when your disabled loved one will take precedence over everyone else; at other times, another family member will take precedence over others.

Fourth, know there is blessing in beginning to develop self-sacrifice. On a few occasions where I was unable to go and participate in an activity, and instead, I stayed home with my daughter. I was able to focus on doing something one-on-one with her, or see her do something that I might otherwise have missed. I have also spent some good quiet time alone that rejuvenated me more than I realized.

Fifth, be thankful for the difficult times. A grateful heart breeds a happy heart. This has not always been the case for me personally. At times, I have had huge pity parties, kicking and screaming, crying, whining, and just feeling sorry for myself and my daughter. I have felt anger toward God and others for my situation. But, the more I thank God for these trying times, the more I am changed from the inside out and realize the blessing in surviving the painful disappointments of life.

Sixth, realize that with time, comes healing. I love this quote from the book, *Jesus Calling*, by Sarah Young,

> ". . . Time is a trainer, teaching you to wait upon Me, to trust Me in the dark. The more extreme your circumstances, the more likely you are to see *My Power and Glory* at work in the situation. Instead of letting difficulties draw you into

worrying, try to view them as setting the scene for My glorious intervention. Keep your eyes and your mind wide open to all that I am doing in your life."

January 6 entry: "Remember, God has our back, in His timing and in His wisdom, He grows us and leads us, learn to trust Him, even in the hard stuff."

Finally, and perhaps the most beautiful aspect of learning to be okay sitting things out is recognizing that someone else around you is also in the same or in a similar situation.

I hear it in someone's tone of voice, I see it written on their face, and I read their body language when they are struggling with difficult things. I understand and can empathize with their position. It is absolutely vital to turn and help someone coming down a similar path behind you.

To be able to look someone in the eye and say, "I know what you are going through," are words of life and healing to someone hurting.

One of my favorite verses in the Bible deals with this beautifully.

> "Praise be to the God and Father of our Lord Jesus Christ, the Father of compassion and the

God of all comfort, who comforts us in all our troubles, so that we can comfort those in any trouble with the comfort we ourselves receive from God. For just as we share abundantly in the sufferings of Christ, so also our comfort abounds through Christ. If we are distressed, it is for your comfort and salvation; if we are comforted, it is for your comfort, which produces in you patient endurance of the same sufferings we suffer. And our hope for you is firm, because we know that just as you share in our sufferings so also you share in our comfort." II Corinthians 1:3-7, NIV

So, you see, compassion is a direct result of dealing with self-sacrifice. Learning self-sacrifice is learning to sit things out and forgo what you want to serve someone else. May we all come to understand that, yes, it is OKAY to sit things out. In fact, it is one of life's most wonderful lessons in order to put yourself in someone else's shoes.

Summary

I recommend a book which helped me personally on my special-needs journey. It is the *Jesus Calling* devotional book by Sarah Young. I have read through the book a few years in a row by just reflecting on each day's short devotional. It has changed my life and my outlook in ways that I cannot even believe. I highly recommend this book for anyone, but especially for those who need comfort. It will bless you.

Several incidents happened at our church involving my daughter with Down syndrome. Two, in particular, stand out most in my mind and in my heart. The first happened a few years ago right after my daughter had first started wearing a bra.

Right after our Sunday morning service was over, I was standing in the side aisle talking with a friend

One-on-One with a Mom of a Special-Needs Child

when I looked up to see Camille walking toward me happily slinging her bra in her hand to give to me. For that one moment, I completely froze with embarrassment. Where had she removed it? Had she taken it off in the foyer or the hallway or the bathroom? Did anyone see her take it off? Had anyone noticed what she was waving around in her hand? She was developing and was around 11 or 12 years old at the time. I was completely mortified!

I quickly came to my senses, grabbed the bra from her hand, and turned around and headed out the side door. I went straight to my car, sat down, closed the door and wept. Yes, I cried and cried. I was so humiliated for me, but also for her. I mean, this was church!

I know that if anyone had noticed what she was doing, I am sure that much of my church family would have totally understood. But, I could just see one little old lady gasping and flabbergasted at her behavior. (Truth be told, I could see my own grandmother, bless her soul, thinking, 'What on earth did you let her do?")

But, I also learned something that day. It is OKAY to cry. It is OKAY to be embarrassed. It is OKAY to be humiliated and humbled. It is OKAY to be different.

Mostly, I realized that it is okay for others to experience something irreverent.

I learned that life happens—the good, the bad, and the ugly. Sometimes it happens to you, and sometimes it happens to me, and you know what? Life goes on. We live and learn, and we are better for all the ups and downs. (However, I still must check before we leave the house to be certain she is wearing a bra!)

The second incident was nothing like the first, but it is one I will remember for the rest of my life. An older gentleman pulled me aside one afternoon at church in our fellowship hall. He had raised a special-needs son years ago.

He looked me straight in the eye and said these words, "I see what you do for your daughter, and you are doing a good job. I see because I know what you do each day, and I care. Most people here at church see what you do, and they care, but they really don't know what you do. People in the world don't really see or know or even care what you do. They say, 'That is your problem.' But, I see, I know, and I care."

Few words were spoken between us, but the impact of this man's thoughtfulness and honesty will remain in my heart for my lifetime. He spoke encouraging, hope-filled, sympathetic words of love which were a sweet balm for my soul.

A Sweet Balm for Your Soul

As you travel on your own special-needs journey, I hope this book will be a sweet balm for your soul. I pray that each of the Six Strategies for Victorious Caregiving and the answers to the questions I have shared will bless you as you experience the good, the bad, and the ugly. Praying, communicating, being thankful and expressing thankfulness, asking for and allowing others to help you, relying on Jesus, and learning self-sacrifice are all keys to your joyful journey.

God has placed you where He wants you to be, and He has surrounded you by good and perfect gifts (James 1:17). We might not always understand God's plans. Ask Him for clarity and how you can live this life for Him. Understand that you have a new normal, and try not to compare your life with the lives of others, especially with those who do not deal with special-needs individuals.

James 1:12 (The Message) says, "Anyone who meets a testing challenge head-on and manages to stick it out is mighty fortunate. For such persons loyally in love with God, the reward is life and more life."

I leave you with two of my favorite quotes and two powerful Bible verses.

From the book, *The Rest of God*, by Mark Buchanan,

> "The Power of the Powerless is Christopher de Vinck's story about Oliver, Christopher's severely mentally and physically handicapped brother. Oliver never spoke a word, never walked a step, never lifted, not once, a spoon to his own lips. His family tended his stick-limbed body like a baby's—fed and bathed and carried and diapered him—from infancy to his death at age thirty-three. Oliver was mute and helpless, but he was a good teacher, he taught the de Vincks that love is not a fluttering, dizzying emotion, gripping you one day, loosing you the next, but a rock-solid resolve to give yourself, day after day after day, to another." Pg. 100

The next quote is from, *The Shack—Reflections for Every Day of the Year*, by Wm. Paul Young.

> "Relationships are never about power, and one way to avoid the will to power is to choose to limit oneself—to serve. Humans often do this—

One-on-One with a Mom of a Special-Needs Child

in touching the infirm and sick, in serving the ones whose minds have left to wander, in relating to the poor, in loving the very old and the very young, or even in caring for the other who has assumed a position of power over them." "Power is about my need to control and, behind that, my insecurity. Help me see with the eyes of the other, to understand sacrifice and resurrection are sisters." April 8 entry.

Romans 12:1 says, "Therefore, I urge you, brothers and sisters, in view of God's mercy, to offer your bodies as a living sacrifice, holy and pleasing to God—this is your true and proper worship.

And finally, I Thessalonians says, 16-18, says,

"Rejoice always, pray continually, give thanks in all circumstances; for this is God's will for you in Christ Jesus."

This unique journey is a blessed one where you learn more and more about mercy, compassion, and love. It is a road less traveled, but it is a path that allows you to experience beautiful gifts that others do not enjoy.

Blessings!

Bobbie Lynn (Brown) Rider

About the Author

Bobbie Lynn (Brown) Rider is married to her best friend, Danny. Together they have 3 grown children. Her oldest daughter is married and works as a nurse along with her husband. Her middle child is currently in college majoring in Marketing. Her youngest was born with Down syndrome and is about to graduate high school. She homeschooled all her children from kindergarten through high school graduation. She holds a Bachelor's degree in Human Ecology, Child and Family Studies and a Master's degree in Higher Education, College Student Personnel from The University of Tennessee.

She is a Sunday school and Ladies class teacher at her church. She has a blog called Grace and Fortitude at www.graceandfortitude.com to encourage Mom's and caregivers of special needs individuals. She enjoys writing, public speaking, hosting Bible studies, crafting/sewing, and serving in various ministry areas.

She is transitioning to an almost empty nest leaving only her youngest as her friend and cohort. It is their desire to encourage others and spread God's love to the world around them.

Manufactured by Amazon.ca
Bolton, ON